I0425862

May 2012

SECURITIES REGULATION

Opportunities Exist to Improve SEC's Oversight of the Financial Industry Regulatory Authority

GAO
Accountability ★ Integrity ★ Reliability

G A O

Accountability * Integrity * Reliability

Highlights

Highlights of GAO-12-625, a report to congressional committees

SECURITIES REGULATION

Opportunities Exist to Improve SEC's Oversight of the Financial Industry Regulatory Authority

Why GAO Did This Study

SEC oversees FINRA, which is charged with regulatory oversight of all securities broker-dealers conducting business with the public in the United States. In light of recent events in the financial markets, SEC and FINRA have faced questions about their oversight roles. The Dodd-Frank Wall Street Reform and Consumer Protection Act required GAO to study SEC's oversight of national securities associations registered under section 15A of the Securities Exchange Act of 1934, a provision which applies only to FINRA. This report examines (1) how SEC has conducted oversight of FINRA, including FINRA rule proposals and the effectiveness of its rules, and (2) how SEC plans to enhance its oversight of FINRA. To address these objectives, GAO reviewed SEC documentation, policies and procedures for inspections of FINRA and reviews of FINRA rule proposals; reviewed documentation on SEC's plans for enhanced FINRA oversight; and interviewed SEC and FINRA officials.

What GAO Recommends

SEC should encourage FINRA to conduct retrospective reviews of its rules and establish a process for examining FINRA's reviews, and SEC should follow all elements of a risk-management framework in developing its future oversight plans. SEC generally agreed with GAO's recommendations.

View GAO-12-625. For more information, contact A. Nicole Clowers at (202) 512-8678 or clowersa@gao.gov.

What GAO Found

Historically, the Securities and Exchange Commission's (SEC) oversight of the Financial Industry Regulatory Authority's (FINRA) programs and operations varied, with some programs and operations receiving regular oversight and others receiving limited or no oversight. Through its inspection process, SEC conducted routine and special inspections of various aspects of FINRA regulatory programs, including examinations, surveillance, and enforcement programs. SEC has also conducted routine inspections of FINRA's advertising and arbitration programs but not as frequently as it had planned. SEC has also regularly reviewed FINRA proposed rule changes that are subject to SEC approval to determine consistency with the Securities Exchange Act of 1934 and related rules and regulations. However, neither SEC nor FINRA conducts retrospective reviews of FINRA's rules. GAO and others have reported on the usefulness of retrospective reviews as they allow agencies to assess the effectiveness of their rules, and some federal financial regulators, including SEC, have begun pursuing plans to conduct retrospective reviews of their rules in light of a recent executive order that encourages independent regulatory agencies to do so. By not conducting these reviews, FINRA may be missing an opportunity to systematically assess whether its rules are achieving their intended purpose and take appropriate action, such as maintaining rules that are effective and modifying or repealing rules that are ineffective or burdensome. Further, by not reviewing what steps FINRA takes in reviewing its existing rules, SEC may not capture sufficient information to form an opinion about FINRA's efforts to review its rules. Further, SEC has conducted limited or no oversight of other aspects of FINRA's operations, such as governance and executive compensation. According to SEC, these operations were not historically considered due to competing priorities and resource constraints. Specifically, SEC officials said that SEC focused its resources on FINRA's regulatory departments, which were perceived as programs that have the greatest impact on investors.

SEC is in the process of enhancing and expanding its oversight of FINRA using a more risk-based approach. To assess the risks facing FINRA, SEC has collected a substantial amount of information on FINRA's regulatory programs and operations, including for programs and operations of FINRA for which it has not previously conducted oversight. SEC has analyzed the information it collected, and, according to SEC staff, will use this information as it implements its enhanced risk-based oversight of FINRA later this year. SEC has followed some elements GAO has previously found to be important in a risk-management framework, but officials have not articulated or documented how they will implement all of the elements, such as considering alternative oversight approaches and monitoring the effectiveness of its oversight. Incorporating these other elements will better position SEC to prioritize evolving and varying risks, evaluate alternatives, and monitor its oversight efforts. Without such elements, SEC may be missing opportunities to take a more comprehensive, risk-based approach in overseeing FINRA.

_____ United States Government Accountability Office

Contents

Abbreviations

COSO	Committee of Sponsoring Organizations of the Treadway Commission
Dodd-Frank Act	Dodd-Frank Wall Street Reform and Consumer Protection Act
Exchange Act	Securities Exchange Act of 1934
FINRA	Financial Industry Regulatory Authority
NASD	National Association of Securities Dealers, Inc.
NYSE	New York Stock Exchange
OCIE	Office of Compliance Inspections and Examinations
SEC	Securities and Exchange Commission
SIFMA	Securities Industry and Financial Markets Association
SRO	self-regulatory organization

United States Government Accountability Office
Washington, DC 20548

May 30, 2012

The Honorable Timothy Johnson
Chairman
The Honorable Richard C. Shelby
Ranking Member
Committee on Banking, Housing, and Urban Affairs
United States Senate

The Honorable Spencer T. Bachus
Chairman
The Honorable Barney Frank
Ranking Member
Committee on Financial Services
House of Representatives

The securities industry is generally regulated by a combination of direct Securities and Exchange Commission (SEC) regulation and industry self-regulation with SEC oversight. Congress adopted self-regulation, as opposed to direct federal regulation of the securities markets, to prevent excessive government involvement in market operations, which could hinder competition and market innovation. Also, Congress concluded that self-regulation with federal oversight would be more efficient and less costly to taxpayers. As regulators, self-regulatory organizations (SRO) such as national securities exchanges and associations, have responsibility for much of the day-to-day oversight of the securities markets and broker-dealers under their jurisdiction. Specifically, SROs are primarily responsible for establishing the standards under which their members conduct business; monitoring the way that business is conducted; and bringing disciplinary actions against their members for violating applicable federal statutes, SEC's rules, and their own rules. SEC oversees SROs to ensure that they are carrying out their regulatory responsibilities. The Financial Industry Regulatory Authority (FINRA), an SRO and the only registered national securities association, has regulatory oversight of all securities broker-dealers doing business with the public in the United States.[1] In particular, FINRA oversees almost 4,500 brokerage firms and approximately 630,000 registered securities representatives and provides regulatory services for approximately 80 percent of the trading volume in U.S. equity markets.

For industry self-regulation to function effectively, SEC must ensure that SROs are fulfilling their regulatory responsibilities. SEC oversees FINRA primarily by inspecting its operations and examination programs and reviewing its proposed rule changes. However, over the last few years, and specifically in light of recent events in the financial markets, SEC and FINRA have faced questions about their oversight roles. These questions include the fairness of FINRA's arbitration practices, the rules it crafts related to oversight of broker-dealers, the limited transparency in its investment practices and corporate governance, and SEC's ability to effectively oversee FINRA.

Section 964 of the Dodd–Frank Wall Street Reform and Consumer Protection Act (Dodd-Frank Act) requires us to review SEC's oversight of national securities associations registered under section 15A of the Securities Exchange Act of 1934 (Exchange Act), a provision that solely applies to FINRA.[2] Specifically, Section 964 identifies several aspects of SEC's oversight of FINRA for our review, including examinations, effectiveness of FINRA's rules, arbitration services, advertising regulation, governance, executive compensation, cooperation with state securities regulators, funding, and policies regarding former FINRA employees. This report examines (1) how SEC has conducted oversight of FINRA, including FINRA rule proposals and the effectiveness of its rules, and (2) how SEC plans to enhance its oversight of FINRA.

To address these objectives, we reviewed and assessed SEC documentation, procedures and guidance for inspections of FINRA. To describe SEC's oversight of FINRA's examination programs and selected services and operations, we evaluated SEC's planning documentation

---

[1]SEC approved the establishment of the Financial Industry Regulatory Authority (FINRA) in July 2007. FINRA is the result of the consolidation of the former National Association of Securities Dealers, Inc. (NASD) (which regulated the over-the-counter market for exchange-listed and nonexchange-listed securities and provided regulatory services to markets such as the American Stock Exchange and the NASDAQ Stock Market) and the member regulation, enforcement, and arbitration operations of NYSE Regulation, Inc.

[2]Pub. L. No. 111-203, § 964(a),124 Stat. 1376, 1910 (2010).

and analyzed SEC's inspection reports from 2005 to 2010 to understand the details of the reviews and the examination areas targeted by SEC. To describe how SEC has overseen FINRA rule proposals, we reviewed and analyzed SEC's documentation on SRO rulemaking policies and procedures, including procedures for approving proposed rule changes. We also interviewed officials from SEC's Division of Trading and Markets (Trading and Markets) as well as FINRA to understand what methods or measures they use to assess the effectiveness of FINRA's rules. To determine what steps SEC has taken or plans to take to enhance its oversight of FINRA, we interviewed officials from SEC's Office of Compliance Inspections and Examinations (OCIE) about plans they have been developing for oversight of FINRA and reviewed OCIE documentation related to these plans. We also reviewed OCIE's preliminary analysis of information collected from FINRA on its regulatory programs and operations related to areas identified in Section 964 of the Dodd-Frank Act, and the extent to which OCIE's plans to enhance its oversight address these areas. We also interviewed other stakeholders such as the Securities Industry and Financial Markets Association (SIFMA) and selected members of SIFMA who are also members of FINRA, as well as a citizen advocacy group. Appendix I contains additional information on our scope and methodology.

We conducted our work from August 2011 through May 2012 in accordance with generally accepted government auditing standards. Those standards require that we plan and perform the audit to obtain sufficient, appropriate evidence to provide a reasonable basis for our findings and conclusions based on our audit objectives. We believe that the evidence obtained provides a reasonable basis for our findings and conclusions based on our audit objectives.

Background

Congress established SEC in 1934 to enforce the Securities Act of 1933 and the Exchange Act. SEC's mission is to protect investors; maintain fair, orderly, and efficient markets; and facilitate capital formation by overseeing key participants in the securities markets, including SROs, securities broker-dealers, investment advisers, and mutual funds. The agency's functional responsibilities are organized into five divisions and 18 offices. Of the 18 offices, OCIE is the largest—with approximately 825 employees—and is responsible for SEC's nationwide examination and inspection program.[3] Individual groups within OCIE have oversight responsibility for SROs, broker-dealers, and investment advisers. OCIE's Market Oversight group examines SROs to ensure that they and their members comply with applicable federal securities laws and SRO rules. As of April 2012, there are 33 employees assigned to the Market Oversight group.

Consistent with its oversight responsibilities for other SROs, SEC is responsible for ensuring that FINRA carries out its regulatory responsibilities related to oversight of broker-dealers.[4] FINRA's responsibilities include registering and examining all securities firms doing business with the public, writing rules and enforcing them, as well as enforcing federal securities laws, and informing and educating the investing public. One of SEC's principal oversight mechanisms for FINRA and other SROs is conducting inspections. Historically, OCIE has conducted both routine and special inspections of SROs. Routine inspections focused on a particular program area during each inspection, based on factors such as the commission's priorities, previously completed inspections, and enforcement actions. Special inspections arose from a tip or a need to follow up on past inspection findings and recommendations. Special inspections have included sweep inspections, whereby OCIE probed specific activities of all SROs it oversees or a sample of them to identify emerging compliance issues.

Another principal oversight mechanism for SEC is its authority to review and, where applicable, approve SRO proposed rules and proposed changes to existing rules, including those submitted by FINRA.[5] Section 19(b)(2) of the Exchange Act, as amended, and related rules and regulations, contain the requirements for SRO proposed rule changes

---

[3]This includes OCIE examination staff in headquarters and regional offices.

[4]In addition to FINRA, SEC oversees more than 20 other SROs, including national stock exchanges, such as the New York Stock Exchange, NASDAQ, and Chicago Options Board Exchange, registered clearing agencies, and the Municipal Securities Rulemaking Board.

[5]Securities Exchange Act of 1934, Pub. L. No. 73-291, 48 Stat. 881 (codified at 15 U.S.C. § 78a *et seq.*).

GAO-12-625 SEC Oversight of FINRA

that are subject to SEC approval.[6] These requirements include that an SRO file a proposed rule change with SEC and publish it on a publicly available website.[7] SEC then sends a notice of the proposed rule change to the Federal Register and allows interested persons the opportunity to submit written comments concerning the proposed rule change.[8] Concurrently, SEC reviews the proposed rule change and, if applicable, considers public comments and the SRO's response. SEC then determines whether the proposed rule change is consistent with the requirements of the Exchange Act and Exchange Act rules and regulations that are applicable to the SRO. SEC has delegated authority to the Trading and Markets Division to approve proposed rule changes.[9] With the passage of the Dodd-Frank Act, SEC can now directly disapprove proposed rule changes that are subject to SEC approval if it does not find that they are consistent with the Exchange Act.[10] SEC also may choose to institute proceedings to determine whether to disapprove a proposed rule change that is subject to its approval if it does not

---

[6]Certain proposed rule changes designated by an SRO pursuant to Section 19(b)(3)(A) of the Exchange Act become effective upon filing and do not require approval by SEC before they go into effect. SEC may suspend the proposed rule change within 60 days of the filing date if it appears to SEC that such action is necessary or appropriate in the public interest, for protection of investors, or in furtherance of the purposes of the Exchange Act. If SEC takes such action, it must institute proceedings to determine whether to approve or disapprove the proposed rule. 15 U.S.C. § 78(b)(3).

[7]The proposed rule change must contain a general statement of its basis and purpose.

[8]SEC must send notice of the proposed rule change to the Federal Register within 15 days of the SRO's website publication date. 15 U.S.C. § 78s(b)(2)(E). The SRO must publish the proposed rule change on its website within 2 business days of filing with the SEC. 17 C.F.R. § 240.19b-4(l).

[9]The Division of Trading and Markets helps SEC maintain fair, orderly, and efficient markets by providing day-to-day oversight of the major securities market participants, such as the securities exchanges, securities firms, and SROs. Its responsibilities include, among others, reviewing proposed new rules and proposed changes to existing rules filed by SROs, assisting SEC in establishing rules and issuing interpretations on matters affecting the operation of the securities markets, and conducting market surveillance.

[10]Prior to the Dodd-Frank Act, SEC could either approve a rule upon an initial review or institute proceedings to determine whether a proposed rule should be disapproved.

approve or disapprove it directly upon its initial review.[11] SEC concludes its review of a proposed rule change by issuing an approval or a disapproval order.[12]

Section 967 of the Dodd-Frank Act directed SEC to engage an independent consultant to examine its internal operations and structure and the need for reform. SEC selected the Boston Consulting Group to conduct the study, and on March 10, 2011, the Boston Consulting Group issued a report on SEC's organizational and operational structure. The study focused on four specific areas: (1) organizational structure, (2) personnel and resources, (3) technology and resources, and (4) relationships with SROs. The study resulted in a report of Boston Consulting Group's findings and recommendations, including some related to SEC's oversight of SROs, and SEC has been working to implement several of these recommendations. Specifically, the report recommended that SEC strengthen its oversight of SROs by developing a set of metrics to assess SRO regulatory effectiveness and suggested that SEC centralize and coordinate its interactions with SROs. SEC has established an SRO working group composed of OCIE and Trading and Markets staff to conduct an evaluation of the current SRO regulatory structure focusing on two areas: (1) disclosures that SROs make, both to the public and SEC, regarding their regulatory operations; and (2) the feasibility of using more defined metrics and standards to assist SEC's oversight of SROs. OCIE and Trading and Markets have also jointly developed a communication plan to help strengthen the oversight of and coordination with SROs and held an outreach conference in January 2012 with all of the equity and options exchanges, the Municipal

---

[11]The proceedings include SEC providing notice and opportunity for a hearing to consider the potential grounds for approval or disapproval, after which SEC makes a final decision by issuing an approval or disapproval order. The Dodd-Frank Act also amended the Exchange Act to extend the period in which SEC must approve or disapprove a proposed rule change or institute disapproval proceedings from 35 to 45 days. However, SEC may extend the period by an additional 45 days if it publishes the reasons for a determination that a longer period is appropriate or the SRO consents to the longer period. Pub. L. No. 111-203, § 916(a) (codified at 15 U.S.C. §78s(b)(2)(A)).

[12]SEC must issue an approval or disapproval order within 180 days of the publication date. However, SEC may extend the period by an additional 60 days if it publishes the reasons for a determination that a longer period is appropriate or the SRO consents to the longer period. If this extension occurs, then SEC has 240 days from the publication date to issue an approval or disapproval order.

Securities Rulemaking Board, and FINRA to discuss issues, such as inspection priorities and the SRO rule filing process.

The Level of SEC's Oversight of FINRA's Programs and Operations Has Varied

SEC's oversight of FINRA's programs and operations varied, with some programs and operations receiving regular oversight and others receiving limited or no oversight. Through its inspection process, OCIE conducted routine and special inspections of various aspects of FINRA regulatory programs, including examinations, surveillance, and enforcement programs. Similarly, Trading and Markets has regularly reviewed FINRA's proposed rule changes to determine compliance with the Exchange Act. However, neither SEC nor FINRA conducts retrospective reviews of FINRA's rules, which would allow them to evaluate the effectiveness of these rules. SEC also has conducted limited to no oversight of other aspects of FINRA's operations, such as governance and executive compensation. According to OCIE officials, the limited or no oversight of these FINRA operations were due to competing priorities and resource constraints. Table 1 summarizes SEC's oversight of FINRA programs and operations identified in Section 964 of the Dodd-Frank Act, which is the focus of our report.

Table 1: SEC's Oversight of FINRA, 2005 to 2010

Areas for SEC oversight of FINRA identified in Section 964 of the Dodd-Frank Act	Frequency of SEC's reviews		
	Annually or continuous[a]	Occasionally[b]	Never
Examinations and expertise of examiners[c]	√		
Advertising	√		
Rules	√		
Arbitration service		√	
Governance		√	
Funding		√	
Post-employment of former employees[d]		√	
Executive compensation			√
Cooperation with states securities regulators			√
Transparency of governance			√

Source: GAO analysis of SEC documentation.

[a]Annually refers to SEC having conducted oversight of this area or some aspects of this area on an annual basis. Continuous refers to SEC reviewing FINRA's rule filings on an ongoing basis.

[b]Occasionally refers to areas for which SEC has not conducted reviews as regularly as it intended or for which it has only reviewed some components of the program or operation.

^cExpertise of examiners is not an area for which SEC has historically conducted oversight, but related issues such as training and staffing have been included in its inspections of FINRA.

^dOCIE formally requested documentation from FINRA related to former FINRA employees and their new employers prior to conducting inspections of FINRA district offices. However, OCIE documented its review of this area in three inspection reports.

OCIE Has Historically Conducted Routine and Special Inspections of FINRA's Regulatory Programs

OCIE has historically conducted routine inspections of various aspects of FINRA's regulatory programs.[13] For example, from 2005 through 2010, OCIE conducted 29 inspections of FINRA district offices—which conduct the majority of broker-dealer examinations—mostly in accordance with a 3-year cycle that existed during that period.[14] In general, these inspections evaluated various FINRA district office regulatory programs, as well as FINRA's efforts to enforce compliance with federal securities laws and FINRA rules. Specifically, during a district office inspection, OCIE would select several FINRA regulatory programs for review. The following describes the type of issues OCIE included in its routine district office inspections of 3 of FINRA's 16 regulatory programs:[15]

- *Routine or cycle examinations*: In its routine inspections of FINRA's examination program, OCIE reviewed FINRA's cycle examinations of broker-dealers to determine whether FINRA district offices met their goals during the period under review.[16] Through its review of FINRA's

[13]Routine inspections are planned inspections for aspects of FINRA but they vary in the frequency with which they are scheduled to be conducted. According to SEC, numerous factors such as commission priorities, risk analysis, and previous inspections play a role in determining the frequency of the inspections.

[14]There are 11 FINRA districts with 15 offices, including Atlanta, Boca Raton, Boston, Chicago, Dallas, Denver, Kansas City, Long Island, Los Angeles, New Jersey, New Orleans, New York, Philadelphia, San Francisco, and Seattle. FINRA's Long Island office, located in Jericho, New York, is a satellite office of FINRA's New York district office. The inspections of FINRA's New York district office included a review of the Long Island office.

[15]The 16 FINRA regulatory programs in the district office inspections included routine or cycle examinations; formal disciplinary actions; the prior national exam program surveillance system; statutorily disqualified persons and member firms; branch office examinations; business gifts, gratuities, and courtesies; financial surveillance; employee securities accounts; subordination loan agreements; membership program; clearing agreements; advertising; new member examinations; automated customer account transfer system; cause examinations; and compliance with municipal rules.

[16]FINRA's cycle examinations are designed to determine whether member firms are in compliance with various SEC, FINRA, and Municipal Securities Rulemaking Board rules and regulations.

examination program, OCIE reviewed district offices' examination scope, completeness of documentation, and analysis of member firms' compliance to determine whether FINRA's review was appropriate.[17]

- *Financial surveillance system*: In its routine inspections of this program, OCIE reviewed FINRA's financial surveillance and whether the district office was periodically monitoring member firms' business activities and financial conditions. In particular, OCIE reviewed whether the reports generated by the surveillance system were adequate and whether the district office used the surveillance data to focus routine examinations on the riskier areas of a firm's business.

- *Formal disciplinary action*: In its routine inspections of this program, OCIE reviewed formal disciplinary actions initiated by FINRA district offices during the period under review. For example, OCIE's inspection assessed whether FINRA district offices' investigations and sanctions were appropriate.

While OCIE selected some programs for review more frequently than others during the period we reviewed (2005-2010), all of FINRA's 16 regulatory programs were reviewed at least once across the 29 district office inspections. We earlier reported that, according to OCIE officials, OCIE tailored inspections in the past to focus on those areas judged to pose the greatest risk to the SRO or the general market, considering such factors as the amount of time that passed since a particular area was last inspected and the results of past inspections.[18] In these inspections, OCIE identified some deficiencies related to FINRA's broker-dealer examinations, such as inadequate documentation, insufficient sampling, and the timeliness of reviews. However, OCIE generally found that FINRA's district offices conducted thorough reviews of their member firms

---

[17]OCIE also previously assessed the quality of FINRA examinations of broker-dealers through its own examinations of broker-dealers that FINRA examined. Although these examinations served as an oversight function, we previously found that they expose firms to duplicative examinations and costs. See GAO, *Mutual Fund Industry: SEC's Revised Examination Approach Offers Potential Benefits, but Significant Oversight Challenges Remain*, GAO-05-415 (Washington, D.C.: Aug. 17, 2005). As a result, OCIE stopped conducting these inspections in 2011.

[18]GAO, *Securities and Exchange Commission: Opportunities Exist to Improve Oversight of Self-Regulatory Organizations*, GAO-08-33 (Washington, D.C.: Nov. 15, 2007).

and that district offices generally addressed deficiencies from the prior inspection.

In addition to the district office inspections, OCIE conducted routine inspections of FINRA's oversight related to advertising. However, these inspections occurred less frequently than what was stated in OCIE's planned inspection timelines.[19] In particular, while OCIE's then existing timelines called for inspections once every 4 years, OCIE conducted inspections of FINRA's advertising regulatory program in 1998 and 2005. According to OCIE, the timelines were not followed due to resource constraints and competing priorities. In the 1998 and 2005 inspections, OCIE reviewed FINRA's assessment of communications submitted by member firms to evaluate their compliance with FINRA advertising rules as well as FINRA's investigation of alleged violations of these rules.[20] In the advertising-related submissions and investigation files reviewed by OCIE in 1998 and 2005, OCIE generally found that FINRA's review met the requirements of FINRA rules, and the OCIE review team did not identify substantial issues with FINRA's oversight of member firms. Although OCIE did not meet their proposed timelines for conducting routine inspections of FINRA's advertising program, our analysis of OCIE's inspections showed that OCIE also reviewed advertising through other efforts, such as including it in some of the FINRA district office inspections previously discussed. Specifically, OCIE reviewed advertising in at least one FINRA district office each year between 2005 and 2010. In those inspections, OCIE reviewed whether the district offices took steps to ensure that customer communications were appropriately reviewed and approved.

OCIE also conducted routine inspections of FINRA's arbitration program. According to OCIE guidance, OCIE planned to conduct inspections of FINRA's arbitration program on a 2-year cycle, but it did not follow this planned schedule. OCIE conducted inspections of FINRA's arbitration program in 2000, 2005, and 2010. The 2000 arbitration program inspection evaluated how FINRA administers various aspects of the

---

[19]FINRA's advertising regulation program is also referred to as the customer communication program in SEC documentation.

[20]For more information on mutual fund advertising and how the regulatory requirements are administered and enforced, see GAO, *Mutual Fund Advertising: Improving How Regulators Communicate New Rule Interpretations to Industry Would Further Protect Investors*, GAO-11-697 (Washington, D.C.: July 26, 2011).

arbitration program including evaluation of the arbitrators, training, and processing of cases, and OCIE found that FINRA generally processed cases in accordance with its guidance. The 2005 inspection, which inspected the New York Stock Exchange's (NYSE) arbitration program that later consolidated into FINRA's arbitration program, identified some deficiencies related to incorrect classifications of some arbitrators, and a lack of sufficient documentation in response to a complaint or negative evaluation regarding an arbitrator. However, OCIE staff found that NYSE either had taken or was taking steps to address these deficiencies. The 2010 inspection of FINRA's arbitration program focused on a sample of FINRA arbitrators, and OCIE's report found that FINRA generally followed its internal procedures related to the qualifications and classifications of its pool of arbitrators. The report also found that FINRA generally removed arbitrators from its roster due to inappropriate conduct or if the arbitrator received credible poor evaluations on a consistent basis.

OCIE has also conducted special inspections—which can arise from tips or the need to follow up on prior recommendations or enforcement actions—of FINRA regulatory programs, as warranted. For example, OCIE inspected FINRA's fixed-income regulatory program in 2006 and was in the process of completing a report for another inspection of this program as of May 2012.[21] Further, due to market conditions, the events of May 6, 2010, also known as the "flash crash," and the dynamic nature of the secondary markets, OCIE has initiated a review of FINRA's surveillance of high-frequency trading.[22] For this inspection, OCIE examiners plan to evaluate the effectiveness of FINRA's automated surveillance programs to detect trading abuses related to high-frequency trading and algorithmic trading. OCIE officials explained that competing

---

[21]OCIE is reviewing FINRA's fixed-income regulatory program, focusing on the effectiveness of FINRA's surveillances in the markups area and also reviewing trade reporting in corporate and municipal fixed-income instruments.

[22]Based on a joint report issued by the Commodity Futures Trading Commission and SEC, on May 6, 2010, the prices of many U.S.-based equity products experienced an extraordinarily rapid decline and recovery. That afternoon, major equity indices in both the futures and securities markets, each already down over 4 percent from their prior-day close, suddenly plummeted a further 5 to 6 percent in a matter of minutes before rebounding almost as quickly. High frequency trading is a subset of algorithmic trading where the high speed with which individuals detect and act on profitable trading opportunities in the marketplace is the defining characteristic. Algorithmic trading is the use of computer and advanced mathematical models to make decisions about the timing, price, and quantity of the market order.

priorities have prevented them from conducting these types of special inspections of SROs on a more frequent basis. Additionally, OCIE conducted other inspections of FINRA (and its predecessor NASD) from 2005 through 2010 that examined other FINRA programs and operations, such as FINRA's anti-money-laundering review program, front-end cause unit, and internal audit department.

Neither SEC nor FINRA Has a Formal Process for Evaluating the Effectiveness of Implemented FINRA Rules

SEC's Division of Trading and Markets regularly reviews FINRA's rule filings and has a formal process in place for its reviews and decisions related to filings. Trading and Markets reviews FINRA proposed rule changes that are subject to SEC approval to determine whether they are consistent with the Exchange Act, and related rules and regulations. During its review, Trading and Markets determines whether a proposed rule change complies with all of the requirements of Form 19b-4—a form that instructs SROs, including FINRA, to provide required information, presented in a clear and comprehensible manner to enable the public to provide meaningful comment and for SEC to determine whether a proposed rule change is consistent with the Exchange Act.[23] If a proposed rule change does not comply with the form requirements, Trading and Markets rejects the filing. If FINRA re-files the proposed rule change and it is complete, Trading and Markets publishes it for public comment.[24] Trading and Markets then determines whether the proposed rule change is consistent with the Exchange Act and, if subject to SEC approval, approves or disapproves it.[25] From 2009 through 2011, SEC issued more than 400 releases regarding FINRA proposed rule changes.[26] We reviewed a sample of 19 of these releases and found that

[23]For example, form 19b-4 requires FINRA to indicate whether the proposed rule change is an initial filing or an amendment to an existing rule as well as whether the proposed rule change is being filed for approval under Section 19(b)(2) or for immediate effectiveness under Sections 19(b)(3)(A) or 19(b)(3)(B).

[24]A complete filing is one that complies with all of the form 19b-4 requirements, the guidelines for publication in the Federal Register, and any requirements for electronic filing as published by SEC (if applicable).

[25]For some proposed rule changes that are subject to SEC approval, SEC can grant approval on an accelerated basis if it finds good cause to do so and publishes the reason for the finding.

[26]SEC releases include rule orders describing SEC's final decision regarding FINRA proposed rule changes and notices.

SEC consistently provided reasons for approving or disapproving proposed rule changes.[27]

Trading and Markets has taken steps to strengthen its review of FINRA proposed rule changes based on recommendations in the Boston Consulting Group study. First, in implementing recommendations from the study, Trading and Markets has developed a more formal structure to consult with OCIE, which has expertise in reviewing and assessing an SRO's regulatory plan and practices. Trading and Markets officials explained that they previously consulted with OCIE on proposed rule changes when necessary but had done so on an informal basis. Second, SEC has also developed an action plan to address other Boston Consulting Group report recommendations, such as plans to provide additional guidance in order to strengthen and clarify the SRO rule filing process. Third, Trading and Markets officials stated that they are formally tracking complex proposed rule changes under review because Section 916 of the Dodd-Frank Act modified certain procedures under Section 19(b) of the Exchange Act, setting tighter time frames for approving proposed rule changes and imposing stricter consequences if deadlines are not met. For example, under Section 916, if SEC does not send a notice to the Federal Register within 15 days of when FINRA posts the proposed rule change on its website, the publication date defaults to the date of FINRA's website posting, which shortens the review period.[28] Prior to the Dodd-Frank Act, Trading and Markets officials stated that they tracked complex proposed rule changes for the Commission on an informal basis. Finally, Trading and Markets assisted in organizing SEC's SRO outreach conference in January 2012 to provide information on, and promote transparency of, the SRO rule filing process.[29]

---

[27]We selected for review 19 SEC releases. Specifically, we randomly selected 2 releases for each year from 2009 through 2011, for a total of 18 releases, from the following categories: releases approving proposed rule changes, releases granting accelerated approval of proposed rule changes, and releases notifying the public of immediately effective proposed rule changes. In addition, we reviewed 1 release disapproving a proposed rule change, the only one for the time period reviewed. For more information on our methodology, please see appendix I.

[28]FINRA posts all of its proposed rule filings on its website within 2 business days of filing with SEC.

[29]Trading and Markets and OCIE conducted an outreach conference in January 2012 to provide information and clarification about the rule-filing process, OCIE's oversight and inspections of SROs, and other similar areas to the SROs SEC oversees.

While SEC reviews FINRA proposed rule changes, it does not have a formal process for conducting retrospective reviews of FINRA rules. Retrospective reviews assess the effectiveness of FINRA rules after they have been implemented. Trading and Markets officials told us that through the process of soliciting comments and conducting reviews of proposed rule changes, SEC gathers information on the potential effects that they may have on the industry. Moreover, according to officials, OCIE may look at a particular rule after approval through targeted or broad examinations of FINRA's operations and services if industry participants or others have raised concerns. For example, OCIE officials stated that in one case, they found that fragmentation in the trading of NASDAQ securities was hindering the ability of the National Association of Securities Dealers, Inc. (NASD)—FINRA's predecessor—to create a complete audit trail and recommended that NASD amend a rule regarding its Order Audit Trail System and require member firms to report complete order information to NASD. However, SEC does not have specific guidance or protocols for conducting retrospective reviews of FINRA's implemented rules.

FINRA also does not have a formal process for conducting retrospective reviews of its rules, but it may review implemented rules informally, according to FINRA officials. FINRA officials stated that there are several mechanisms that they employ in their routine oversight activities that could be used to evaluate the effectiveness of implemented rules. These mechanisms include soliciting feedback from FINRA's Board of Governors and industry organizations, analyzing customer complaints and arbitration claims, and performing examination and oversight functions related to member and market regulation. FINRA officials also stated that they review existing rules when there are new industry developments. Further, FINRA officials stated that the ongoing consolidation between the NASD and NYSE rulebooks—which was part of FINRA's creation in 2007—provides an opportunity to evaluate the effectiveness of existing FINRA rules. However, without a more formal process in place to examine its implemented rules, FINRA might miss opportunities to consistently evaluate the effectiveness of its rules. Further, SEC currently does not have a process by which it reviews what steps FINRA takes in reviewing its existing rules, which could result in SEC not capturing sufficient information to form an opinion about FINRA's efforts to review its rules. OCIE staff is currently reviewing how FINRA's regulatory programs evaluate the effectiveness of FINRA's rules and how FINRA's rulemaking process helps to ensure the effectiveness of its rules.

Recently, federal financial regulators have been encouraged to conduct retrospective reviews of existing rules. In 2011, the President signed Executive Order 13579, which asked independent regulatory agencies, such as SEC, to develop plans for reviewing existing significant regulations.[30] The order encourages these agencies to conduct retrospective reviews of their rules in order to modify or repeal rules that may be ineffective, insufficient, or excessively burdensome. We and others have also reported on the usefulness of retrospective reviews of rules, including their ability to inform policymakers about the design of rules and regulatory programs.[31] Although the financial regulators are not required to follow Executive Order 13579, SEC is developing plans for conducting retrospective reviews of its rulemaking. Specifically, SEC has issued a Federal Register notice soliciting public comments to assist the agency in developing plans for conducting retrospective reviews in response to the executive order.[32]

While Executive Order 13579 does not apply to FINRA, its regulatory responsibilities are similar to those of federal financial regulators.[33] Specifically, FINRA proposes many rules and rule changes each year in its regulatory role of overseeing broker-dealers and the markets in which they operate. These rules can have an impact similar to those proposed and implemented by financial regulators, such as SEC. Thus, the Executive Order could provide SEC criteria to encourage FINRA to conduct retrospective reviews of its rules. By not conducting retrospective reviews of its rules, FINRA may be missing an opportunity to assess whether its rules are achieving their intended purpose.

---

[30]Independent regulatory agencies are those defined by 44 U.S.C. § 3502(5).

[31]GAO, *Reexamining Regulations: Opportunities Exist to Improve Effectiveness and Transparency of Retrospective Reviews,* GAO-07-791 (Washington, D.C.: July 16, 2007)

[32]Section 610 of the Regulatory Flexibility Act requires independent and other regulatory agencies to review within 10 years of publication any of their rules that have a significant economic impact on a substantial number of small entities. Pub. L. No. 96-354, §3(a), 94 Stat. 1164, 1169 (1980) (codified at 5 U.S.C. § 610).

[33]FINRA is an SRO, incorporated in Delaware as a nonprofit entity, and is therefore not an independent regulatory agency.

OCIE Has Conducted Limited or No Oversight of Other Aspects of FINRA's Operations

OCIE has conducted limited oversight of some aspects of FINRA's operations, as described below.

- *Governance*: SEC has not directly overseen FINRA's governance but has monitored structural changes of the Board of Governors to ensure that policies and rules related to governance are being appropriately followed. For example, SEC and FINRA officials told us that OCIE has periodically reviewed the composition of FINRA's board to determine compliance with SRO board-composition requirements.[34] Through its authority to review FINRA rule filings, Trading and Markets also reviews new rules or proposed changes to existing rules related to corporate governance or other governance-related issues. However, SEC has not historically examined issues such as conflicts of interest or recusals related to FINRA's governance.

- *Funding*: Although OCIE has not examined the sufficiency of FINRA's funding in the past, OCIE officials told us that they have reviewed FINRA's annual report and any relevant information to understand FINRA's finances. For example, OCIE has reviewed this information to determine whether FINRA needs more resources in certain areas, such as training. OCIE officials have not historically focused on the adequacy of FINRA's funding because of competing priorities and resource constraints.

- *Employment of former FINRA employees at regulated entities*: OCIE's guidelines for inspections of FINRA district offices included information about examining FINRA examiners who had terminated their employment. In addition, according to OCIE officials, inspections of district offices typically include a review of issues related to former FINRA employees. For example, from 2005 through 2010, OCIE formally requested documentation from FINRA related to former FINRA employees and their new employers prior to conducting inspections of FINRA district offices. OCIE officials provided three inspection reports that documented that this issue was examined in the inspections during this period.

---

[34]FINRA's governance structure is outlined in its by-laws, which among several qualifications include diverse industry representation of three small, one medium, and three large firms. In 2006, OCIE conducted a special inspection of the NASD Board of Governors election based on a complaint. In its review, OCIE found that NASD generally conducted its election in accordance with its legal obligations and did not find any deficiencies that its staff believe would have changed the outcome of the election.

OCIE has not historically conducted oversight of some areas of FINRA's programs and operations identified in Section 964, including FINRA's executive compensation, cooperation with state securities regulators, and transparency of FINRA's governance. Specifically, OCIE officials told us that they focused their limited resources on FINRA's regulatory departments which they perceived as programs that have the greatest impact on investors. However, as will be discussed, SEC is currently re-evaluating its oversight of FINRA, including the levels of oversight dedicated to aspects of FINRA's programs and operations that it has not historically overseen.

SEC's Efforts to Enhance Oversight of FINRA Could Benefit from Following All Elements of a Risk-Management Framework

OCIE is in the process of enhancing and expanding its oversight of FINRA using a more risk-based approach. In 2010, OCIE transitioned from conducting routine, or cycle-based, inspections of the SROs it oversees, including FINRA, to a more risk-based approach to oversight. We have previously reported that, according to OCIE officials, in the past OCIE tailored inspections to focus on areas with the greatest risks and considered the results of past inspections and other factors in planning routine inspections.[35] However, OCIE continued to conduct inspections on a cycle-basis. With the transition to a more risk-based inspection process, OCIE officials stated that they are working to focus their resources on the most critical and high-risk areas in their oversight of FINRA and other SROs, rather than continuing to conduct cycle-based inspections. To assess the risks facing FINRA and conduct reviews of FINRA programs, OCIE collected a substantial amount of information on FINRA's regulatory programs and operations, including those for which it had not previously conducted oversight but which Section 964 of the Dodd-Frank Act identified. OCIE has analyzed the information it collected, and, according to OCIE officials, will use this information as it implements its enhanced risk-based oversight of FINRA later in 2012. While OCIE has followed some elements of a risk-management framework as it has considered its existing and future oversight of FINRA, it has not addressed all elements of the framework. For example, OCIE officials have not articulated or documented how they will select the appropriate alternatives for enhanced oversight and how they will monitor the implementation of OCIE's oversight. Without doing so, OCIE may be missing opportunities to take a more comprehensive approach to

---

[35]GAO-08-33.

considering all risks and alternatives associated with oversight of FINRA, as well as the monitoring of its future efforts.

OCIE Is Assessing FINRA's Risks as Part of Its Efforts to Enhance and Expand Oversight of FINRA

With the goal of enhancing its oversight of FINRA, OCIE is working to assess potential risks FINRA faces. These risks may also affect SEC's general oversight of the securities industry, and more specifically, how SEC will oversee FINRA. To assess potential risks FINRA faces, OCIE has obtained information and data on various aspects of FINRA's regulatory programs and operations. This includes information on FINRA's examinations of broker-dealers, its surveillance programs, arbitration, advertising regulation, and governance. It also has collected information from FINRA's internal audit reports, and reports prepared by third parties for FINRA.[36] OCIE officials said that they focused their information collection efforts on the areas identified in Section 964 of the Dodd-Frank Act because these were the risks that Congress identified.

OCIE officials have analyzed the information they collected for different FINRA programs and operations, including areas that they have previously overseen.

- **Examinations**. According to OCIE's preliminary analysis of the information collected, OCIE has analyzed the number of examinations FINRA has conducted of member firms as well as the number of examiners that FINRA employed between 2008 and 2010. OCIE has also been reviewing several aspects of FINRA's examination programs to further develop its risk-based approach, including how FINRA communicates with its members and SEC about its examination programs. For example, according to OCIE's analysis, OCIE staff are reviewing the extent to which FINRA's examination process is transparent to its member firms and SEC. OCIE staff are also reviewing how FINRA is filling open examiner positions with well-qualified applicants, and how FINRA trains its examiners. To assess how FINRA has filled examiner positions with well-qualified applicants, OCIE obtained data on recently hired staff in FINRA's examination program, staff turnover rates, criteria that FINRA uses in

---

[36]FINRA's internal audit department uses a risk-based approach in developing its plan for audits of FINRA regulatory programs and operations over a 4-year cycle. The approach includes annual risk assessments that assess various types of risks, such as financial and regulatory risks, and the internal controls related to FINRA programs and operations.

determining experience levels of its staff, and guidelines on how FINRA staffs examinations. OCIE also obtained information, such as job descriptions, that outlines education and experience requirements for examiner positions. According to OCIE officials, this information will be used to develop a systematic review of examiner expertise in future inspections of FINRA. OCIE officials are also reviewing how FINRA compensates and trains its examiners, including whether FINRA assesses the adequacy of examiner compensation.

- **Arbitration**. According to OCIE's analysis, OCIE staff are reviewing FINRA's documentation and procedures related to arbitrator selection. In addition, OCIE staff are examining staffing levels, staffing changes, and staff compensation in FINRA's dispute resolution department and FINRA's procedures for monitoring trends in case filings. OCIE staff are also reviewing information regarding FINRA's procedures for establishing performance benchmarks for its arbitration program, such as the time to serve claims and appoint arbitrators.

- **Advertising**. OCIE staff are reviewing FINRA's funding of its advertising regulation department to determine whether it is receiving adequate funding to sufficiently implement, administer, and staff FINRA's advertising review program. OCIE staff have conducted preliminary analysis on how many member filings each analyst in FINRA's advertising regulation department is expected to review, the turn-around time for filings, the number of filings submitted relative to the number of staff reviewing them, and supervisory reviews of analysts' work. According to OCIE officials, this analysis is designed to inform future, risk-based inspections of FINRA's advertising program and target areas that warrant the most attention.

OCIE also collected information on aspects of FINRA's operations for which OCIE has historically conducted limited or no oversight but which Section 964 of the Dodd-Frank Act identifies. These aspects include oversight related to FINRA's governance, cooperation with state securities regulators, policies regarding former FINRA employees, executive compensation, and funding.

- **Governance**. According to OCIE's analysis, OCIE staff are reviewing information board members receive from FINRA management in carrying out their duties and the extent to which governance practices are transparent. OCIE staff are examining the process by which FINRA governors recuse themselves from matters that raise a potential conflict of interest. According to OCIE staff, they are also examining other governance-related issues, such as independence and fiduciary duties and the expertise and skill sets of FINRA governors.[37]

- **Cooperation with state securities regulators**. OCIE staff have been reviewing the extent to which FINRA communicates effectively with state securities regulators. OCIE staff are also exploring whether any opportunities exist for improving cooperation between FINRA and state securities regulators, as OCIE recognizes the importance of enhanced communication between FINRA and state securities regulators. Such communication could become even more important if FINRA becomes an SRO for investment advisers. Although there are many variations of what an investment advisor SRO could look like, one scenario is that FINRA could share examination authority over certain investment advisers with state regulators alone rather than with state regulators and SEC, as is currently the case with broker-dealers.

- **Post-employment policies regarding former FINRA employees**. OCIE staff have been reviewing FINRA's written procedures concerning former employees and comparing FINRA and SEC post-employment restrictions to assess whether FINRA could implement additional controls. OCIE staff are also examining policies that FINRA has adopted and take effect in July 2012 that place restrictions on former FINRA officers, such as vice presidents, senior vice presidents, and higher-ranking FINRA executives. These restrictions would prevent a former FINRA officer from appearing in a FINRA disciplinary proceeding for 1 year following the date of that officer's separation from FINRA.

- **Executive compensation**. OCIE has obtained information and data on FINRA executive compensation, including retirement plans and incentive compensation for its executives. OCIE staff have been reviewing the data, specifically focusing on compensation FINRA pays its senior executives and the annual goals set by FINRA's Management Compensation Committee. These goals include those that FINRA senior executives must meet to qualify for incentive compensation and the analysis and deliberations undertaken by FINRA, the Management Compensation Committee, and FINRA's

---

[37]FINRA's Board is comprised of governors representing various groups and interests, such as small, mid-size, and large firms; investment companies; and the public.

Board of Governors in connection with the award of incentive compensation. According to OCIE's analysis, OCIE officials are also reviewing the firms or entities that FINRA uses for compensation benchmarking purposes and examining studies conducted by FINRA's compensation consultant.[38] We reviewed the three most recently completed compensation studies conducted by the consultant—in 2009, 2010, and 2011—and found that these studies concluded that FINRA's pay levels are appropriate relative to certain comparable regulators, exchanges, and financial services organizations engaged in brokerage or related banking.

- **Funding**. As part of its analysis, OCIE officials are examining FINRA's annual budget process among other funding-related items. In particular, officials observed budget discussions and interactions during FINRA's annual planning process between FINRA's operating departments and divisions, FINRA's Financial Planning and Initiatives team (which develops FINRA's budget), senior management, the Finance and Operations Committee, and the Board of Governors. Further, officials are reviewing FINRA's Board of Governors' oversight of the budgeting process. OCIE officials have also been assessing issues concerning FINRA's investment portfolio, such as FINRA decisions related to levels of portfolio contributions to annual spending. In addition, OCIE officials are reviewing FINRA's management of investment-related conflicts of interest. Finally, as part of its monitoring of FINRA's resource allocation, OCIE officials are assessing FINRA's plans to fund an investment adviser oversight program and how FINRA would maintain sufficient funding to fulfill its current core regulatory programs relating to broker-dealers. FINRA has indicated an interest in becoming an SRO for investment advisers if Congress were to approve legislation permitting the creation of one or more SROs for investment advisers.

OCIE's analysis of the information collected on FINRA's programs and operations is ongoing. OCIE officials anticipate using the information they have collected and analyzed to inform their planning of future oversight of FINRA. According to OCIE officials, implementation of OCIE's enhanced, risk-based FINRA oversight will begin later in the year.

---

[38]Since 2004, FINRA has retained the services of a consultant to conduct a review each year to provide the Management Compensation Committee with ongoing guidance concerning competitive executive compensation pay levels, overall compensation program structure, and other related compensation matters.

OCIE's Methodology for Developing Enhanced, Risk-Based Oversight of FINRA Could Benefit From More Closely Following a Risk-Management Framework

While OCIE is engaged in efforts to develop and implement an enhanced risk-based approach to oversight of FINRA, its approach does not follow all the elements of a formal risk-management framework. According to OCIE staff, they developed the framework for their risk-based approach, in part, by considering the Committee of Sponsoring Organizations of the Treadway Commission's (COSO) enterprise management framework.[39] COSO's enterprise risk-management framework contains eight components for managing risk: internal environment, objective setting, event identification, risk assessment, risk response, control activities, information and communication, and monitoring. However, OCIE officials explained that they modified this framework to focus on three elements: (1) risks facing FINRA, (2) internal controls FINRA has in place to mitigate those risks, and (3) the residual risks that are not mitigated by the existing internal controls. OCIE officials explained that they decided to modify the COSO framework, in part, to customize the process to OCIE's needs and expertise.

In prior work, we have reported on the benefits of risk management and identified elements of a risk-management framework for federal agency oversight efforts.[40] Risk management provides the rigor and structure necessary to enable entities, on a continuous basis, to enhance their capability to identify potential adverse events, assess risks, and establish appropriate responses. Figure 1 shows the five elements for a risk-management framework, which are also described below. All of these are critical to OCIE's efforts to develop an enhanced risk-based inspection program.

- **Identify strategic goals, objectives, and constraints** refers to identifying the strategic goals that are trying to be achieved and the steps needed to attain those goals. It also includes determining limitations or constraints that affect the desired outcomes.

---

[39]COSO was organized in 1985 to sponsor the National Commission on Fraudulent Financial Reporting, an independent private-sector initiative that studied the causal factors that can lead to fraudulent financial reporting. It also developed recommendations for public companies and their independent auditors, for SEC and other regulators, and for educational institutions, including frameworks and guidance on enterprise risk management.

[40]GAO, *Risk Management: Further Refinements Needed to Assess Risks and Prioritize Protective Measures at Ports and Other Critical Infrastructure*, GAO-06-91 (Washington, D.C.: Dec. 15, 2005).

- **Risk assessment** refers to identifying the key aspects of potential risk.
- **Alternatives evaluation** refers to considering measures to reduce the identified risks.
- **Management selection** refers to management selecting where resources and investments will be made based on selecting the appropriate alternatives for reducing risks.
- **Implementation and monitoring** refers to how the steps to reduce risk will be applied and monitored to help ensure ongoing effectiveness.

Figure 1: Elements of a Risk-Management Framework

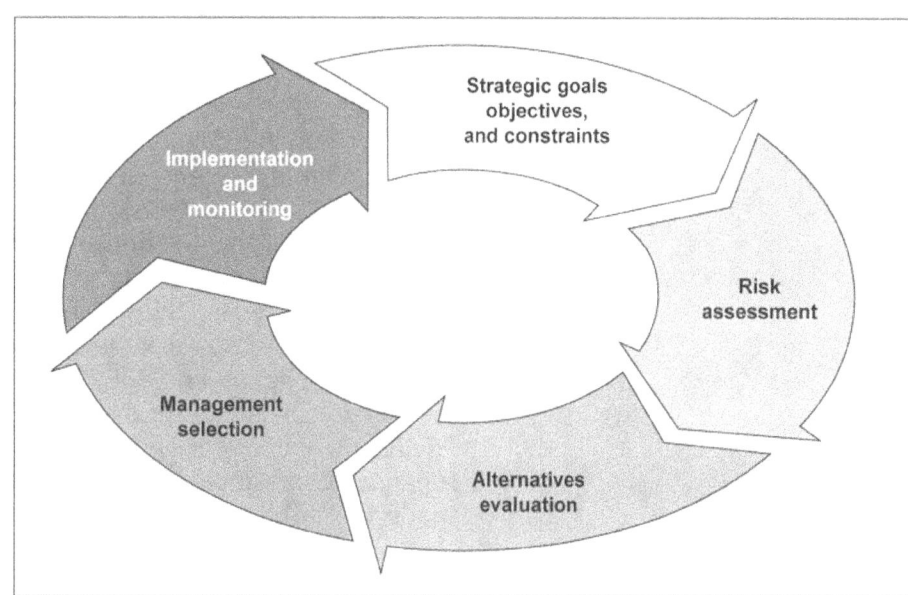

Source: GAO.

While these elements are designed for agencies overseeing their own risks and programs, they can be applied to SEC's oversight of FINRA and its efforts to enhance its oversight. To oversee the securities markets, SEC leverages its own capabilities as well as those of the SROs it oversees, including FINRA. For example, SEC relies on FINRA for examinations of broker-dealers and in instances where SEC and FINRA pursue joint enforcement actions. As such, the risks associated with FINRA's surveillance programs and its oversight of broker-dealers potentially affect SEC's ability to effectively regulate the securities markets. Specifically, FINRA's regulation of its members and its surveillance activities serve as crucial oversight functions, on which SEC relies. A failure of FINRA's oversight is a risk to SEC and its ability to fulfill its mission. Therefore, for SEC to conduct effective oversight of the securities markets, it must take steps to ensure that FINRA is performing these functions properly.

OCIE has taken steps to incorporate the first two elements of the risk-management framework. OCIE has identified its goals and objectives—specifically, enhancing oversight of FINRA—and is assessing FINRA's potential risks. As previously mentioned, OCIE plans to develop an oversight plan based on its risk assessments and will focus on the risk areas determined to be the highest risk. To inform its oversight plan, OCIE plans to conduct risk assessments on a regular basis. For example, OCIE has already imbedded procedures for identifying risks related to FINRA's regulatory programs in its district office inspection procedures.

However, while OCIE officials have addressed two of the five elements, they have not articulated or documented how they plan to implement the remaining three elements of the risk-management framework: considering alternatives for reducing risks; selecting the appropriate alternatives for enhanced oversight; and implementing and monitoring its risk-based oversight. While OCIE officials may have initiated internal discussions about these elements, they have not formally presented specific steps for them, nor are all three elements apparent in the modified risk-management approach OCIE adopted. Because these elements are not formally articulated, OCIE may not be in the best position to determine whether its staff are actively considering how to implement and monitor enhanced oversight of FINRA once the key risks are identified and prioritized.

The remaining three elements of the risk-management framework could also provide SEC with other opportunities to improve its oversight efforts. For example, the areas identified in Section 964 of the Dodd-Frank Act may not contain an equal amount of risk, and that risk may vary over time. As such, SEC must continuously identify and prioritize these evolving risks in order to appropriately target its resources. Further, the FINRA programs and operations identified in Section 964 may not encompass all current and future risks. For example, should FINRA become the SRO for investment advisers, SEC would need to consider the potential impact of FINRA's additional responsibilities and reassess risks related to FINRA's current oversight of broker-dealers and its surveillance functions. Moreover, as we have previously recommended, leveraging the findings in FINRA's internal audits is another important source of information that SEC could use to assess current or evolving risks.[41] Establishing all elements of a risk-management framework would provide SEC with a comprehensive plan to develop the appropriate options to identify current and future risks, including those not specifically identified in Section 964 of the Dodd-Frank Act, prioritize them, and implement an oversight plan that can be monitored for effectiveness. Without such elements, OCIE may be missing opportunities to take a more comprehensive approach to considering all risks and alternatives associated with oversight of FINRA, as well as the monitoring of its future efforts.

Conclusions

SEC has a formal process for reviewing FINRA's proposed rule changes and has recently taken steps to strengthen its review process. However, neither FINRA nor SEC has a formal process for evaluating the effectiveness of FINRA's implemented rules. Increasing attention has recently been given to the importance of these retrospective reviews and some federal financial regulators, including SEC, have begun pursuing plans to conduct retrospective reviews of their rules. Although FINRA also publishes rules governing the securities markets, it is not required to conduct such reviews of its rules. However, given its role in regulation, FINRA proposes many rules and rule changes each year that can have an impact similar to rules proposed and implemented by SEC. By not conducting retrospective reviews, FINRA may be missing an opportunity to systematically assess whether its rules are achieving their intended purpose and take appropriate action, such as maintaining rules that are effective and modifying or repealing rules that are ineffective or burdensome.

SEC is in the process of enhancing and expanding its oversight of FINRA, using a more risk-based approach. To inform these plans, SEC has worked to assess the risks associated with the FINRA programs and operations. Moving forward, incorporating the other elements we have previously identified for a comprehensive risk-management framework will be important, including prioritizing risks and monitoring the effectiveness of its oversight. For example, although SEC collected information on all FINRA programs and operations identified in Section 964 of the Dodd-Frank Act, the risks posed by the individual programs and operations could vary and therefore warrant different levels of

---

[41]GAO-08-33.

oversight. Moreover, the FINRA programs and operations identified in Section 964 may not encompass all current and future risks, such as FINRA becoming an SRO for investment advisers. Incorporating these other elements of the risk management framework will better position SEC to identify and prioritize evolving risks, evaluate alternatives and monitor its oversight efforts. Without such elements, SEC may be missing opportunities to take a more comprehensive, risk-based approach in overseeing FINRA.

Recommendations for Executive Action

As SEC works to enhance its oversight of FINRA, we recommend that the SEC Chairman take the following two actions:

- encourage FINRA to conduct retrospective reviews of its rules and establish a process for examining FINRA's reviews; and
- direct OCIE to follow all elements of a risk-management framework as it develops plans for an enhanced risk-based approach to FINRA oversight, such as developing plans for how it will prioritize risks related to oversight of FINRA and assessing the effectiveness of its risk-based model.

Agency Comments

We provided a draft of this report to SEC for review and comment. In its comment letter, which is reprinted in appendix II, SEC generally agreed with our recommendations. Pursuant to our first recommendation concerning retrospective reviews of rules, the SEC Chairman has requested that OCIE and Trading and Markets encourage FINRA to consider additional methods to conduct these reviews. The Chairman has also requested that OCIE consider the most effective method to examine or monitor FINRA's reviews of its rules. In response to our second recommendation that OCIE follow all elements of a risk-management framework, SEC commented that they had planned to do so and agreed that implementation of the remaining elements of a risk-management framework may better position OCIE to take a more comprehensive, risk-based approach in overseeing FINRA. As such, OCIE will consider how best to prioritize evolving and varying risks, evaluate alternatives, and monitor oversight efforts related to its oversight of FINRA. SEC also provided technical comments on the draft report, which we incorporated as appropriate.

We also provided portions of the draft report to FINRA for review and comment. FINRA provided technical comments, which we incorporated as appropriate.

We are sending copies of this report to the Chairman of the Securities and Exchange Commission, the appropriate congressional committees, and other interested parties. In addition, the report will be available at no charge on GAO's website at http://www.gao.gov.

If you or your staffs have any questions about this report, please contact me at (202) 512-8678 or clowersa@gao.gov. Contact points for our Offices of Congressional Relations and Public Affairs may be found on the last page of this report. GAO staff who made major contributions to this report are listed in appendix II.

A. Nicole Clowers
Director, Financial Markets and Community Investment

Appendix I: Scope and Methodology

The objectives of this report were to examine (1) how the Securities and Exchange Commission (SEC) has conducted oversight of the Financial Industry Regulatory Authority (FINRA), including FINRA rule proposals and the effectiveness of its rules, and (2) how SEC plans to enhance its oversight of FINRA.

To address our first objective, we reviewed and assessed SEC documentation, procedures, and guidance for inspections of FINRA. To describe how SEC has conducted oversight of FINRA's examination programs specifically, we reviewed and assessed SEC's Office of Compliance Inspections and Examinations' (OCIE) procedures and guidance for inspections of FINRA's examination programs, including OCIE's guidelines for oversight inspections of FINRA district offices, inspection planning memorandums, and advertising inspection checklists. We analyzed all (29) of OCIE's inspection reports of FINRA district offices for inspections conducted from 2005 to 2010 to understand the details of the reviews, including the scope and findings of the inspections. Additionally, we reviewed other OCIE inspection reports related to aspects of FINRA oversight identified in Section 964 of the Dodd-Frank Wall Street Reform and Consumer Protection Act of 2010 (Dodd-Frank Act), including the 1998 and 2006 inspections of the National Association of Securities Dealers, Inc.'s (NASD) Department of Advertising Regulation, 2000 inspection of NASD Dispute Resolution's Midwest Regional Office, 2002 inspection of NASD's surveillance program for member-firm trading in municipal securities, and 2006 inspection of NASD's regulatory program for fixed-income securities. We also reviewed relevant documentation OCIE collected from FINRA, including FINRA's member regulation handbook, samples of letters FINRA sends to firms to discuss various regulatory issues, and questionnaires FINRA uses in its meetings with member firms when conducting oversight examinations. We reviewed request letters SEC submitted to FINRA for inspections that SEC had recently initiated of FINRA's surveillance programs related to fixed income and high-frequency trading. We also interviewed SEC, FINRA, and North American Securities Administrators Association officials. Moreover, we interviewed other relevant stakeholders such as the Securities Industry and Financial Markets Association (SIFMA), members of SIFMA who are also members of FINRA, and a citizen advocacy group. SIFMA assisted us in identifying members who varied in size—small, medium and large—and had been in existence prior to the creation of FINRA in 2007. We also reviewed relevant prior GAO reports regarding SEC oversight of FINRA and self-regulatory organizations (SRO) in general.

To describe how SEC has overseen FINRA's proposed rule changes and what methods or measures SEC and FINRA use to assess the effectiveness of FINRA's implemented rules, we reviewed and analyzed SEC's documentation on SRO filing policies and procedures, including SEC procedures for approving proposed rule changes, relevant federal statutes governing SEC's review of SRO rule filings, and recent executive orders regarding retrospective reviews of existing regulations. We also interviewed officials from SEC's Division of Trading and Markets, FINRA, members of SIFMA who are also members of FINRA, and we reviewed prior GAO reports on agencies conducting retrospective reviews of existing rules.

To understand the steps SEC takes to review and approve or disapprove FINRA's proposed rule changes, we analyzed a random sample of SEC releases regarding FINRA's proposed rule changes issued in 2009, 2010, and 2011.[1] We selected the years 2009 through 2011 because these were the most recent years that contained a full year of releases and included a full year of releases before and after the enactment of the Dodd-Frank Act. We examined SEC releases approving proposed rule changes, granting accelerated approval of proposed rule changes, notifying the public of immediately effective proposed rule changes, and disapproving proposed rule changes.

1. Approved: Proposed rule changes from SROs, including FINRA, that were filed for approval under section 19(b)(2) with approval occurring after the 30th day of the publication date (date of the Federal Register publication or SRO website posting).

2. Accelerated approval: Amendments to previously filed proposed rule changes from SROs, including FINRA, that were filed for approval under section 19(b)(2) with approval occurring before the thirtieth day of the publication date (date of the Federal Register publication or SRO website posting).

3. Immediately effective: Certain categories of proposed rule changes from SROs, including FINRA, that were filed for immediate effectiveness under section 19(b)(3)(A). Categories include (i) rules constituting a stated policy, practice, or interpretation with respect to

---

[1]SEC releases include rule orders describing SEC's final decision regarding FINRA proposed rule changes and notices.

the meaning, administration, or enforcement of an existing rule, (ii) rules establishing or changing a due, fee, or other charge imposed by the self-regulatory organization on any person, or (iii) rules concerned solely with the administration of the self-regulatory organization or other matters specified by SEC.

4. Disapproved: Proposed rule changes from SROs, including FINRA, that were filed for approval under Section 19(b), but were disapproved.

We obtained a list of all SEC releases regarding FINRA proposed rule changes from SEC's website for the years 2009 through 2011, a total of 432 releases. We identified all approved, accelerated approval, immediately effective, and disapproved release types issued during the 3 years and randomly selected two occurrences for each type of release for each year. There was only one occurrence of a disapproved release available on SEC's website for the time period of 2009 through 2011.The result was a nongeneralizable sample of 19 SEC releases (18 approved, accelerated approval, and immediately effective releases and 1 disapproved release) that we examined to understand how SEC reviews FINRA proposed rule changes and arrives at its decisions. We reviewed the releases based on elements we identified from SEC's SRO rule filing statute, including SEC allowing for public comments and explaining its rationale for the decision to approve or disapprove a proposed rule change.

To address our second objective, we reviewed OCIE documentation of plans they have been developing for oversight of FINRA, and we interviewed officials from OCIE about these plans. We also reviewed documentation on OCIE's preliminary analysis of information collected from FINRA on its regulatory programs and operations related to areas identified in Section 964 of the Dodd-Frank Act, and the extent to which OCIE's plans address these areas. We also reviewed other SEC documentation on its plans for enhanced oversight, including risk analysis plans for future inspections of FINRA, scoping memorandums for areas of oversight identified in Section 964 of the Dodd-Frank Act, and information and data requests SEC sent to FINRA regarding these areas. We also reviewed SEC documentation on the implementation of SEC organizational reform recommendations identified in a study conducted by the Boston Consulting Group of SEC's structure and operations. To assess SEC's risk-based oversight framework, we reviewed literature and documentation on the Committee of Sponsoring Organizations of the Treadway Commission's enterprise management framework. We also reviewed guidance and documentation on the elements of risk-management frameworks and prior GAO work on models or frameworks related to agency oversight efforts.

We conducted our work from August 2011 through May 2012 in accordance with generally accepted government auditing standards. Those standards require that we plan and perform the audit to obtain sufficient, appropriate evidence to provide a reasonable basis for our findings and conclusions based on our audit objectives. We believe that the evidence obtained provides a reasonable basis for our findings and conclusions based on our audit objectives.

Appendix II: Comments from the Securities and Exchange Commission

UNITED STATES
SECURITIES AND EXCHANGE COMMISSION
WASHINGTON, D.C. 20549

DIVISION OF
TRADING AND MARKETS

OFFICE OF COMPLIANCE
INSPECTIONS AND EXAMINATIONS

May 22, 2012

A. Nicole Clowers
Director
Financial Markets and Community Investment
U.S. Government Accountability Office
441 G Street, NW
Washington, DC 20548

Dear Ms. Clowers:

Thank you for the opportunity to review the Government Accountability Office's (GAO) draft report concerning the SEC's Oversight of the Financial Industry Regulatory Authority. The SEC staff is separately providing you with technical comments on the draft report.

GAO prepared the draft report in response to Section 964 of the Dodd-Frank Wall Street Reform and Consumer Protection Act, which requires GAO to review the Commission's oversight of FINRA in a number of substantive areas. As you know, the Financial Industry Regulatory Authority (FINRA) plays a critical role in monitoring and regulating activities in the securities industry. The SEC, in turn, operates a robust program for the oversight of FINRA. Specifically, as noted in the draft report, the SEC's oversight of FINRA is primarily conducted by the Office of Compliance Inspections and Examinations (OCIE) through its risk-based inspection and examination process and the Division of Trading and Markets (DTM) through its review of FINRA proposed rule changes.

As we discussed during GAO's review, OCIE conducted a critical self-assessment of its inspection and examination process, adopting a risk-based methodology, including developing a new risk-based approach for FINRA. Since 2010, OCIE has enhanced and expanded its oversight of FINRA. As part of this enhanced FINRA oversight, OCIE analyzed extensive information from FINRA and conducted numerous interviews of senior management, key personnel and members of FINRA's Board of Governors regarding numerous areas, including areas not articulated in Dodd-Frank Section 964.

GAO makes two recommendations in the draft report regarding the SEC's oversight of FINRA. First, the draft report recommends that the SEC encourage FINRA to conduct retrospective reviews of its rules as well as establish a process for examining FINRA's reviews of its rules. With respect to this recommendation, the Chairman has requested that OCIE and DTM encourage FINRA to consider additional methods to conduct retrospective reviews of its rules to

A. Nicole Clowers
May 22, 2012
Page 2

assess whether FINRA's rules are achieving their intended purpose. In addition, the Chairman has requested that OCIE consider the most effective method to examine or monitor FINRA's review of its rules.

Second, the GAO's draft report recommends that OCIE consider all elements of a risk-management framework when developing future FINRA oversight plans. These elements include: 1) identifying goals and objectives for enhancing oversight of FINRA; 2) assessing FINRA's potential risks; 3) considering alternatives for reducing risks; 4) selecting the appropriate alternatives for enhanced oversight; and 5) implementing and monitoring our risk-based oversight.

We appreciate that GAO acknowledged that since 2010 OCIE has effectively implemented the first two critical elements of the GAO's risk-management framework for enhanced FINRA oversight. While noting that OCIE is still finalizing its enhanced risk-based oversight of FINRA, GAO's draft report recommends that OCIE incorporate the remaining three elements of a risk-management framework. We had planned to do so, and agree with the GAO recommendation that the implementation of the remaining elements of a risk-management framework may better position OCIE to take a more comprehensive, risk-based approach in overseeing FINRA. In this regard, OCIE will consider how best to prioritize evolving and varying risks at FINRA, including those not articulated in Dodd-Frank Section 964. OCIE also will consider how best to evaluate alternatives and monitor our oversight efforts. We anticipate that as we conclude our current review of FINRA later in 2012, we will work to implement effectively the remaining three elements of a risk-management framework described in the draft report.

We appreciate the GAO's attention to these important issues and would like to thank you and your staff for the opportunity to review the GAO's draft report.

Sincerely,

Carlo di Florio
Director
OCIE

Robert W. Cook
Director
Division of Trading and Markets

Appendix III: GAO Contact and Staff Acknowledgments

GAO Contact	A. Nicole Clowers, (202) 512-8678 or clowersa@gao.gov
Staff Acknowledgments	In addition to the contact named above, Andrew Pauline (Assistant Director), Vida Awumey, Chir-Jen Huang, Jonathan Kucskar, Tarek Mahmassani, Marc Molino, Luann Moy, Jessica Sandler, and Jennifer Schwartz made key contributions to this report.

GAO's Mission	The Government Accountability Office, the audit, evaluation, and investigative arm of Congress, exists to support Congress in meeting its constitutional responsibilities and to help improve the performance and accountability of the federal government for the American people. GAO examines the use of public funds; evaluates federal programs and policies; and provides analyses, recommendations, and other assistance to help Congress make informed oversight, policy, and funding decisions. GAO's commitment to good government is reflected in its core values of accountability, integrity, and reliability.
Obtaining Copies of GAO Reports and Testimony	The fastest and easiest way to obtain copies of GAO documents at no cost is through GAO's website (www.gao.gov). Each weekday afternoon, GAO posts on its website newly released reports, testimony, and correspondence. To have GAO e-mail you a list of newly posted products, go to www.gao.gov and select "E-mail Updates."
Order by Phone	The price of each GAO publication reflects GAO's actual cost of production and distribution and depends on the number of pages in the publication and whether the publication is printed in color or black and white. Pricing and ordering information is posted on GAO's website, http://www.gao.gov/ordering.htm. Place orders by calling (202) 512-6000, toll free (866) 801-7077, or TDD (202) 512-2537. Orders may be paid for using American Express, Discover Card, MasterCard, Visa, check, or money order. Call for additional information.
Connect with GAO	Connect with GAO on Facebook, Flickr, Twitter, and YouTube. Subscribe to our RSS Feeds or E-mail Updates. Listen to our Podcasts. Visit GAO on the web at www.gao.gov.
To Report Fraud, Waste, and Abuse in Federal Programs	Contact: Website: www.gao.gov/fraudnet/fraudnet.htm E-mail: fraudnet@gao.gov Automated answering system: (800) 424-5454 or (202) 512-7470
Congressional Relations	Katherine Siggerud, Managing Director, siggerudk@gao.gov, (202) 512-4400, U.S. Government Accountability Office, 441 G Street NW, Room 7125, Washington, DC 20548
Public Affairs	Chuck Young, Managing Director, youngc1@gao.gov, (202) 512-4800 U.S. Government Accountability Office, 441 G Street NW, Room 7149 Washington, DC 20548

Please Print on Recycled Paper.